COMMANDER JOHN KERANS
1915-1985

First published in 2001 by
Short Books
15 Highbury Terrace
London, N5 1UP

ISBN 0 571 20825 8

Printed in Great Britain by
Bookmarque Ltd, Croydon, Surrey

LAST ACTION HERO OF THE BRITISH EMPIRE

COMMANDER JOHN KERANS

1915-1985

NIGEL FARNDALE

✳ SHORT BOOKS

For Samuel

16 Goda Road,
Littlehampton,
Sussex,
England

May 2, 1949

My darling John,

I wonder if you have any idea of my thoughts these past ten days since you took command of the Amethyst? I felt it might be tempting providence too much to put pen to paper. Now I can listen to the news bulletins without that ghastly feeling inside! I want you to know, my darling, how very proud I was, and am, that you were chosen for the job. My pride in you vies very much with my anxieties. I wonder when you'll realise how often your name and photograph appear on the front page of a vast number of newspapers?!

Your wife and daughter have been basking in your reflected glory and even our little poppet has her picture on the front page of at least three papers... I know how excited you must be about your new command. The Sunday Empire News refers to you as a brilliant young naval officer hand-picked for the job. I do hope you won't hate it all, darling; after all, it's very nice publicity and I insisted on restraining those reporters from including mush and slop. The thing that bothers me is that they appear to make seven years difference in age between us. They've nearly all got you as 35 and the stupid Daily Express puts me at 28, without having asked! Anyway, what is it to anyone how old we are? The news tonight says you have been advised by Chinese Communists to stay put for the time being.

Darling, you asked of Charmian. She talks well with quite an extensive vocabulary. She says her prayers each night and now adds, with the initial prompting from me, 'Please God, bring Daddy safely home.' She will have it that you're on a 'nasty old boat' – I've told her 'ship' but she prefers 'boat'.

Well, good night, darling, my thoughts and prayers are for you constantly.

All my love, from your ever loving wife,

Stephanie

Twelve days earlier.
Nanking, China.

Having spent half of his 16 years' commissioned service in Far East waters, Lieutenant Commander John Simon Kerans had become a reluctant connoisseur of Chinese food. The 16-course banquets he was expected to attend, in his capacity as Assistant Naval Attaché to the British Embassy at Nanking, were always something of an ordeal. But on the evening of Wednesday 20 April 1949, as he buffed his shoes and flicked dust off his dress uniform in preparation for yet another feast – hosted on this occasion by Admiral Kwei Yung-chin, the Commander-in-Chief of the Nationalist Chinese Navy – he found his appetite had deserted him completely.

He was brooding over a 'flash' signal (one which takes priority over all others in the air) that he had been handed a few hours earlier. The signal had been sent to 'all ships' from the First Lieutenant of HMS *Amethyst*, a Royal Navy frigate that had been sailing up the grey-brown tidal waters of the Yangtse river to relieve HMS *Consort*, the guardship at Nanking.

'Under heavy fire', the flash read. 'Am aground in approx. position 31 degrees 10 minutes North 119 degrees 50 minutes East. Large number of casualties.' It was indeed 'approx.', as these co-ordinates placed the ship several miles inland – a surreal twist to an unnerving message.

In the spring of 1949, China was at war with itself. The Communist army, led by Mao Tse-tung, had swept down from the northern plains of the country and was now gathering on the banks of the Yangtse, waiting to cross. The Nationalists, led by Chiang Kai-shek, were still nominally in power, and their forces were massed around the capital, Nanking, on the opposite bank of the river. The Yangtse – a fast-flowing natural obstacle that varied in width from one to 20 miles and stretched 3,400 miles, from the mountains of Tibet across the whole of central China and out to the East China Sea – had become, in effect, a no man's land, the front line of battle.

On that fateful Wednesday, John Kerans had been told by his superior, Captain Vernon Donaldson, the Naval Attaché, that he should attend the banquet – so that it wouldn't look as if the British were rattled by what was already becoming known as the 'Yangtse Incident'. He was then to report to the Embassy for a briefing immediately afterwards. It proved to be a tense dinner, with both the British and the Chinese guests pretending nothing was wrong. Conversation was interrupted by constant telephone calls for the Chinese Admiral, who was, no doubt, being briefed about the *Amethyst* situation. And every few minutes, the dining-room was plunged into darkness – the Nationalist Chinese Navy was bombarding the Communist Chinese positions nearby, and this was affecting the electricity supply.

Later, back at the Embassy, Kerans joined Donaldson and the Acting Military Attaché, Major Raymond Dewar-Durie (D-D as he was better known), for an emergency meeting with the British Ambassador, Sir Ralph Stevenson. All agreed that it was an outrage for the Communists to attack a foreign neutral warship in waters where rights of passage had long been recognised. As best they could, they tried to establish exactly what had happened and why.

According to the latest information received from the *Amethyst*, at 9.30am that morning, 20 April, a shell had whipped over the 300ft, 1,430-ton frigate from starboard, the side of the river held by the Communists, and plunged into the water. Four shells had followed in quick succession and hit three separate and vital parts of the ship. The *Amethyst* had returned fire. Soon afterwards, the bridge had taken two direct hits and everyone up there had been killed or wounded, including the captain, Lieutenant Commander Bernard Skinner. The order 'full astern on both engines' had come too late and, with the port engine stopped and her starboard engine at full speed, the *Amethyst* had driven her bows firmly into the mud bank, 150 yards from the western shore of Rose Island – where she was a sitting target for the Communist guns. Some 37 dead or wounded still lay on the deck – while 20 more wounded had been landed on shore and were being sent by the Nationalist Chinese to a nearby hospital.

Imbued with the bullish confidence of the Senior Service and steeped in the traditions of gunboat diplomacy, HMS *Consort* had steamed off from Nanking to help the *Amethyst,* but she, too, had come under fire and, after suffering eight men killed, 30 wounded and 56 direct hits, she had had to leave the scene. HMS *Black Swan*, a frigate, had then tried to reach the *Amethyst* from the other direction, sailing upriver from the sea, but Communist shells had claimed seven of her crew and she, too, had had to turn back. The cruiser HMS *London* had also tried to rescue the frigate but, after losing 13 men, and with 14 seriously wounded, she, too, had been driven back, the hidden shore batteries having gained the advantage in the battle.

The Ambassador had a diplomatic crisis on his hands. As an emergency measure, he decided to send Kerans to Chinkiang, an ancient walled city set in a half-circle of hills a few hundred yards from the banks of the Yangtse, and just downriver from HMS *Amethyst's* last reported position. Kerans's orders were to investigate the reports, ensure the well-being of the wounded at the hospital in Chinkiang and, if possible, to make contact with the ship.

Because D-D could speak the local language, he was to be sent along, too. Kerans was told to obtain a supply of medical stores, especially morphine, and D-D was to take plenty of Chinese money from the British Embassy, in case it was needed for bribes. They were also given 2,000 cigarettes, a crate of beer, Chinese Admiralty charts of the Yangtse, and a letter from Admiral Kwei Yung-chin saying that all Nationalist Chinese concerned were commanded to give the British officers any help they requested. They would set off first thing the next morning.

***

In truth, 33-year-old Kerans was probably the last officer in the Royal Navy that the Admiralty would have chosen – if they had had a choice – for this particular walk with destiny. In the months and years to come, Kerans would be fêted, mythologised even, as a national hero. Parades would be held in his honour, mothers would name their children after him and, in a feature film, he would be played by that chisel-jawed matinee idol Richard Todd. Yet, when he was entrusted with this dangerous and diplomatically sensitive mission, our man was languishing in a desk job, without any further prospect of promotion, in a forgotten outpost of the Empire, because he was seen by the Admiralty as a liability.

This had not always been the case. As a young officer,

Kerans had shown not only great promise but also flashes of brilliance. He had thrived on the challenge and excitement of combat and had proved himself extremely courageous in battle. Even the bravest of men have their limits, though, and, by 1945, Kerans bore some deep psychological scars. In peacetime, his career had faltered. He found life boring, drank too much and became accident-prone, erratic and, at one particularly low point, he had faced the ignominy of a court martial.

John Kerans was a lean man, straight-spined, 5ft 11in tall. His face was long, his eyes green and his ears small and pinned close to his head. Tattooed on his right forearm was a Chinese dragon, the legacy of a much-regretted drunken night in Hong Kong when he was a 17-year-old midshipman. His hair was dark brown, straight and brushed back, and he had tight-reddish skin and a sharp, aquiline nose always aimed above the horizon.

His main pleasures in life came from pink gin, cigarettes (which he chain-smoked) and the music of Tchaikovsky. Although his temper was short and he had a reputation for aloofness – which may have been born of shyness – his sense of humour was dry and he could be charming, when occasion demanded. As he put it, he 'could dance just well enough not to be conspicuous'. His shipmates put his mercurial nature down to his Irish temperament. For although he spoke laconically, with the refined voice of one educated at an English public school, he had been born, on 30 June 1915, in Birr, Kings County, Ireland.

Bravery seems to have been a family trait. His father, Edward, was an officer in the Worcestershire Regiment and won a DSO in the First World War – as did his uncle, Charles Kerans, who served with the Indian Medical Service. His brother, Patrick, who was three years his junior, also served in the Worcesters and won five medals posthumously, after being killed in the assault on Keren during Field Marshal Wavell's campaign against the Italians in Abyssinia.

John was 11 when his father died – as a result of being gassed in the First World War. Two years earlier, Major Kerans had been posted to Belfast. At that time, John was a boarder at Tibberton Court, a prep school in Gloucester, so this posting effectively meant that father and son never really got to know each other.

At the age of 13, inspired by *Boy's Own* stories of heroism on the high seas, Kerans decided to break with the family tradition of joining the Army and applied instead for a cadetship at the Royal Naval College, Dartmouth. He was ordered to meet the other 43 boys in what was named the 'Drake Term', the January 1929 intake, at Paddington station. Shivering in the chill winter winds, each boy eyed the others' parents for social solecisms. All were in their new naval caps, which were far too large for them, and their British warm overcoats – all, that is, except Kerans. He was in civilian clothes because he hadn't had time to visit Gieves, the naval outfitters. In fact, he hadn't made it through the selection process: another candidate had died from typhoid and so he had received a last-minute telegram telling him to join. Nevertheless, to scrape in was still an achievement: for every boy offered a place at Dartmouth, six were rejected.

The young recruit had his first culture shock after unpacking his trunk in the dormitory: he was told to 'lay at attention' in bed. The college ran a harsh regime: boys had to rise at 6am, dive naked into an icy, over-chlorinated plunge bath, stand to attention in front of the basins awaiting the order 'wash necks' followed by 'wash teeth'. At 6.10am the order came to 'get dressed' followed five minutes later by 'say prayers'. After breakfast came square-bashing on the parade ground followed by studies and, after lunch, games.

John Kerans hardly shone at Dartmouth. He wound his way through 11 terms without achieving any notoriety or promotion to cadet captain. He played wing three-quarter at rugby, and was accomplished at swimming, tennis and squash, and he won cups for fencing and sprinting. But he was usually in the bottom quarter academically, and received many canings for minor infringements, on one occasion for not folding his clothes properly. Being late, being slack, or not having a button or a shoelace done up was always punished with the cane, and this punishment was called 'Guff'. More serious crimes, such as smoking and drinking, were punished with 'Official Cuts'. Somewhere between lay a punishment known as 'Strafes'; this was for lack of 'Term Spirit', a mysterious quality – something to do with being clubbable – which was never properly defined.

Despite all this, Kerans was usually cheerful and sometimes cynical about the whole Dartmouth curriculum. His reports described him as 'a good mixer' and noted that he was liked by his fellow students, even if some regarded him as 'a bit of a joke'.

What mattered most, as far as the college was concerned, was that, while still in their adolescence, cadets acquired a veneer of manhood. The unofficial principle behind the regime was that a graduating officer wouldn't find war nearly so harsh as college. Whenever Kerans or his peers felt wobbly, they could take inspiration from the inscription on the College war memorial: 'See that ye hold fast to the heritage we leave you, yea, and teach your children its value that never in the coming centuries their hearts may fail them or their hands grow weak.'

By the outbreak of the Second World War, Kerans had reached the rank of Lieutenant and was in Singapore, on the staff of the Chief of Intelligence, Far East. Fearing he might miss the action, he requested a transfer to Atlantic convoy duty, an almost thankless task as, in one three-month period alone, German U-boats sank 300 merchant ships.

In the winter of 1940, he was serving in HMS *Naiad*, a cruiser, when she was sent to Jan Mayen Island to destroy a German weather station and a trawler known to be arriving there (thanks to the Enigma codebreakers at Bletchley Park). By steaming fast through mountainous seas and drift-ice, the ship arrived in time to meet the Germans. The *Naiad* trained her guns on the trawler. She then lowered her motor cutter, with Kerans in command, and an armed party and plenty of explosives were towed astern in a whaler. Kerans succeeded in capturing the Germans in the trawler and then set fire to the weather station. After he had unloaded half the prisoners on board the *Naiad*, he returned to the island for the remainder, but the swell increased and the whaler 'broached to' in the icy surf. While he worked out a way to get back to the ship, he ordered the captured Germans, as well as the British sailors left ashore, to do physical jerks to keep themselves warm. He eventually got his motor cutter close enough for the party to wade out to him. For this action, he was mentioned in despatches by Admiral of the Fleet Sir Charles Forbes.

Some weeks later, in January 1941, when the *Naiad* was several hundred miles west of the Orkneys, a sharp-eyed seaman boy, who was one of the lookouts, spotted smoke on the horizon. It was confirmed by the ship's navigating officer as well as by Kerans, the officer of the watch. Aware of intelligence reports that the *Scharnhorst* and her sister ship the *Gneisenau* were about to break out into the Atlantic and attack Allied shipping, Kerans – without first consulting the captain – ordered 'action stations', altered course towards the smoke and rang the engine-room to order 'full speed'. As the throttles were opened, the turbine hum rose to a high-pitched whine.

When Rear Admiral ELS King, the admiral flying his flag aboard the *Naiad*, reached the bridge, he demanded to know what was happening. He surveyed the horizon with his binoculars and, unable to see any smoke himself, cancelled the chase. A few minutes later, *Naiad*'s sister ship, HMS *Phoebe*, reported that she had seen two blips on her radar on the same bearing as Kerans had seen the smoke. Admiral King now had to swallow his pride and order the chase to begin again at maximum speed – but it was too late. Vital time had been lost and, after an eight-hour dash, he gave up.

On return to Scapa Flow, Kerans was reprimanded for acting precipitately. A subsequent Board of Inquiry decided the ship had 'gone off on a wild goose chase'. It was not until after the war, when the German archives were opened up, that it was discovered the sighting had indeed been of the *Scharnhorst* and the *Gneisenau*. Their more sophisticated radars had spotted the British flotilla and they had turned at full speed (which caused the puff of smoke seen by the lookout). The two German battle-ships went on to destroy 120,000 tons of shipping before reaching Brest. With justification, Kerans felt he had been treated unfairly in this matter, but at the time of the incident he bowed to the verdict of the Inquiry and bit his lip. This was uncharacteristic behaviour because he usually spoke his mind and was rarely tactful to spare someone's feelings. The fact that he always questioned authority was probably one of the things that held him back in the Navy.

The greater part of Kerans's war service was in the Mediterranean, much of it in the hard-fought Malta convoys. In one convoy alone, the *Naiad* and other ships endured 287 enemy-bomber attacks. But it was during the evacuation of Crete in May 1941 that Kerans was to experience the event that would change his life forever.

The *Naiad*'s sister ship, HMS *Orion*, had just sailed from the island, crammed with soldiers, when she was successfully dive-bombed. The casualties were huge – 300 were killed on one mess deck alone. The *Orion* limped back to Alexandria for repairs, and it was Kerans's horrific task to take charge of the working party who, with the stench of death filling their nostrils, literally had to dig out the dismembered remains of bodies. He was traumatised by this and, according to one officer who knew him at the time, he never fully recovered.

By this stage of the war, some of the crew of HMS *Naiad* were becoming shell-shocked – or 'bomb happy' as it was known – but it was noticeable that Kerans remained eerily calm. As his friend Louis le Bailly, an engineer officer in *Naiad*, who later became a vice-admiral, noted: 'It was rudely suggested that John was sub-normal and became normal only when the rest of the crew were becoming hysterical. The *Orion* experience bit deeply into him. But he could keep his head while all about him were losing theirs. He was an unimaginative man but a very brave one.'

On 11 March 1942, northwest of Sollum off Crete, HMS *Naiad* was sunk. After an air attack that had lasted from 9am to 6.30pm, the cruiser had had the misfortune to encounter a lone U-boat. A torpedo hit her amidships and, as she heeled to starboard, the order 'abandon ship' was given. Kerans had a choice of jumping from the low side of the ship, where he might be crushed if the ship rolled on top of him, or taking the high side, where the barnacles and bilge keels might lacerate him as he dropped. He opted for the latter and survived unscathed, unlike many of his comrades. The sea was rough but not too cold as Kerans swam frantically away from the sinking *Naiad* to avoid its suction. From a safe distance, he watched the cruiser's bows rear up before she sank back into the depths. He and the other survivors near him gave a small cheer. They had been through a lot together with that ship.

Their ordeal wasn't over yet, though. There was little hope of rescue because any destroyers in the area would be hunting for the U-boat in order to protect the rest of the squadron – and everyone knew it was unwritten Navy procedure to depth-charge enemy submarines regardless of the consequences for their own survivors in the water. With his life-jacket holding him up, Kerans closed his eyes, resigned himself to his fate, and waited for sleep to bear him away.

After an hour, a destroyer, HMS *Jervis*, hove into view. Kerans swam with the other men towards the scrambling-nets hanging over its side, but on arrival he barely had the strength to haul himself up.

Understandably, the strain of war now began to show. The sinking of the *Naiad* was merely the latest in a long line of traumas: Kerans's father had died just before he was subjected to the harsh regime at Dartmouth; his brother had been killed just before he went to fight in a war in which he, too, would be bombed constantly; worst of all, standing knee-deep in mutilated bodies on the deck of HMS *Orion*, he had witnessed a Dantesque vision of Hell. Something, it seemed, had changed in Kerans's neural make-up. He had become emotionally atrophied; almost autistic. Nowadays he would probably be diagnosed with Post-Traumatic Stress Disorder, offered compensation and visited by teams of trauma counsellors. In those days, the only remedy offered was a stiff drink.

His spirits lifted – temporarily – after he met Stephanie Campbell Shires, an attractive, urbane and good-humoured officer in the WRNS. Their first encounter was at Combined Operations HQ Portsmouth, during the preparations for D-Day in 1944: she was working as a Plotting Officer, he was temporarily attached to the Movements Office (much to his disgust because he would have preferred to have been at sea).

After D-Day, the Wrens held a party. John Kerans was invited by one of Stephanie's girlfriends, who had a crush on him. The feeling wasn't mutual, however, and, while dodging Stephanie's friend, he bumped into Stephanie. They danced and chatted and he told her he was feeling very chipper because he had just been given his first command – of HMS *Blackmore*, a Hunt-class destroyer. She told him about her family home in Tavistock, Devon, and the job she had had before the war, working at the National Central Library.

But the couple didn't really stay in touch after the party and Stephanie started dating a naval dentist. Just before John Kerans sailed for Italy he wrote to Stephanie from his club, the Naval and Military, in Piccadilly: 'By the next time I see you, you will probably be the mother of several little toothrights!' He seemed to have reconciled himself to coming second in Stephanie's affections.

On *Blackmore*'s first trip up to Scapa Flow she got entangled in the boom. All harbours were protected by booms and nets in wartime to keep out enemy submarines; they were opened, closed and maintained by boom-defence staff. A couple of weeks later, just off Sheerness, she had to be rescued again, having got a cable wrapped round her propeller. She spent the night flashing her light at shipping until divers freed her next day. It was not an auspicious start to Kerans's first command. Back at the Admiralty, black marks were beginning to appear against his name.

Kerans's interpersonal skills were sometimes less than ideal. As his navigating officer in HMS *Blackmore*, Alan Tyler, recalled: 'Kerans had started drinking heavily as an escape from the strain of war. He did not carry it well. He sometimes returned onboard the worse for wear and had to be helped to bed, which was embarrassing for the duty officer and bad for morale. He was also not a great ship handler, nor an easy man to work with. You never knew how he was going to react. Ours was not a happy ship.'

Stephanie, meanwhile, had been posted to Colombo, Ceylon, to work on Operation Zipper, the campaign to retake Malaya from the Japanese. She was dealing with the reinforcement of ships and, when she saw that HMS *Blackmore* was one of them, she decided to get in touch again with Kerans. She wrote a note: 'Obviously I have not had the time to become the mother of several little toothrights! And my dentist friend has gone out to the British Pacific Fleet...' John Kerans was based at Trincomalee on the other side of the island. She hitched a lift over to him in a Beaufighter and, after a few days, they got engaged. Later, when Kerans's mother, Eva, met Stephanie, she said to her: 'Are you sure, dear? Do you know what you're taking on? John can be very difficult you know.'

At the end of the war, the *Blackmore* was sent home as part of the inevitable reduction of the huge wartime fleet – only the best and most modern ships were to be kept manned. But the destroyer was to be involved in another rescue incident before she retired. On 23 October 1945, a Board of Inquiry was held aboard HMS *Myngs* to determine the cause of the grounding of HMS *Blackmore* on 12 October. Kerans was awarded their Lords' (Admiralty) displeasure.

At Christmas time, all regular servicemen were

awarded a month's 'End of War leave'. Kerans made the most of his by getting married to his fiancée. In order to comply with the rules of residence for marriage, the couple used the address of a cousin of Stephanie, who had a flat in Plymouth. They married in St Mathias's Church there on 7 January 1946. Stephanie found a wedding cake and John was able to produce some alcohol from his ship, but, because of rationing, the wedding was a spartan affair. The honeymoon was a rainy week in Tintagel on the north Cornish coast. Stephanie hoped she would be able to join her husband on his next posting abroad, but it wasn't to be and this left her feeling 'a little bitter'. On 3 March he wrote from his ship, which was just off Gibraltar: 'Stephanie my darling, How dreadfully lonely it feels without you. I simply hated my final departure.But there it is. It had to be...'

Later that year, on 7 October, a daughter, Charmian, was born. Kerans was in Hong Kong at the time and didn't hear the news for two days. He sent a letter back asking what time Charmian had been born, adding that the idea of buying a pram sounded 'top-hole' and that he wouldn't be home for a long time yet. When Stephanie read it, while still in a nursing home with the baby, she burst into tears. John Kerans also sent a telegram to his daughter: 'Dear Charmian, Welcome into this great universe. Hope we meet some day soon. Love and blessings from your father.'

Husband and wife wrote to each other once a week – and Stephanie teased John about always writing 'man's letters. Very to the point. Not what you would call good love letters.' But, she supposed, they had probably been censored. By now, after repeated mishaps, Kerans could no longer be considered as a man marked out for greatness in the Navy. But the worst – or, as it turned out, the most fortuitous twist in his career – was yet to come. In 1947, having reached the rank of Lieutenant Commander, he was given command of a frigate, HMS *Widemouth Bay*. Perhaps for inspiration, he kept in his cabin a framed photograph of himself in boxing shorts and gloves posing by a trophy. One night, while the ship was berthed in the dockyard at Malta, several members of his crew returned from a heavy drinking session on shore and proceeded to urinate over the side of the ship; then, laughing boisterously, they stripped naked and jumped into the harbour. Unfortunately, this happened in full view of the admiral superintendent of the dockyard, who was on his veranda hosting a cocktail party. The admiral's guests thought it some kind of cabaret. There was a Board of Inquiry at which it was suggested that Kerans himself had been one of the high-spirited officers involved; there was also speculation that his crew had turned mutinous, stripped him and thrown him into the water. This charge was not pursued, but, on 8 October 1947, a court martial did find Kerans guilty on two other counts: of accepting as a present six bottles of alcohol from the wardroom officers; and of being negligent in the performance of his duty when he had allowed all but one of his officers to remain on leave for an extra day after the ship's company had been due to re-embark.

So it was that in April 1949 Lt Cdr John Kerans found himself in a dead-end job in Nanking, poised to prove to the Admiralty that he was exactly the right officer in the right posting at the right moment in history.

***

At first light on the morning of Thursday 21 April 1949, John Kerans went in search of transport for his journey to Chinkiang. The British Embassy had no cars that worked, but word got out among the diplomatic community in Nanking and the Australian Military Attaché offered to lend his old jeep. At 10am, Kerans and Major Dewar-Durie set off on their 72-mile journey. A major and a lieutenant commander are equivalent in rank but, as this was a naval operation, Kerans was in charge. D-D was in battledress and Kerans, not knowing what to expect and thinking he would be away for a few hours only, was in his blue winter uniform and a Burberry raincoat (he didn't have so much as a toothbrush with him by way of personal belongings). He was feeling exhilarated. In career terms, he had little to lose and everything to gain from this rescue mission.

The jeep travelled 100 yards before it broke down. After they had kicked and shaken the vehicle for a few minutes, it started again. The breakdowns continued regularly on their jolting, three-hour journey over dusty, potholed roads. Chinkiang was still thronged with Nationalist soldiers in their drab, olive-green cotton uniforms and puttees, padding in soft-soled cotton shoes along cobbled streets. But the civilians were beginning to flee before the Communist onslaught, blocking the roads out of the city with their hand-carts laden with pots, clothes and chickens in cages. On arrival, Kerans made for the sector headquarters of the Nationalist Chinese Navy, a grand, grey-brick house near the riverfront. Here he met Captain 'Mark' Meh, a British-trained Chinese officer who spoke English well. Meh was soon able to dispel the report that 20 British wounded had arrived in Chinkiang – most of the wounded were still onboard, he said, and the ship was still afloat. In his clipped, well-modulated voice, Kerans requested a craft to take him out to the *Amethyst*. In his pidgin English, Meh explained that there wasn't one available.

On an antique telephone with ringing handle, Kerans then called Donaldson, the Naval Attaché in Nanking. 'There doesn't seem to be anything you can do,'

Donaldson said. 'You'd better come back.' Shortly afterwards, Donaldson rang to tell Kerans that he had just received a signal from Geoffrey Weston, the First Lieutenant of the *Amethyst*, to say that he would be trying to move further upriver that night. Kerans should try to get to the ship before dark. The American Embassy would lend a doctor, Donaldson added, one Lieutenant Commander J W Packard, and Kerans should wait for him at Chinkiang before setting off in search of the *Amethyst*.

Without a boat, Kerans and his party had no option but to reach the stricken vessel by land. He asked Meh for a guide, as well as a couple of trucks for the wounded. Meh was able to supply these, along with a letter of passage from General Wang, the Nationalist commander in the area. By now caught up in the excitement, Meh asked if he could come along too.

At 3.30pm, a large American car arrived bringing Packard, a burly figure in a fur-collared, windproof jacket. Three-quarters of an hour later, the American doctor, the British officers and the Chinaman set out in an Australian jeep in search of the ship. Under a mild April sun, they followed a route that took them along the southern fringe of hills that range parallel with the Yangtse. The country here, among groves of bamboo and mulberry, is low-lying and marshy. Coolies under huge straw hats, carrying wooden yokes across their shoulders, jumped aside as the jeep drove past. The road soon became loose stones and mud, and was so badly potholed it looked heavily shelled. It took two and a quarter hours to cover just 23 miles. Finally, at 6.20pm, as the party arrived at the headquarters of the 177th (Nationalist Chinese) Regiment, near Ta Chiang, the road came to an end. The trucks for the wounded could go no further. Kerans decided that this should be the assembly-point for the rescue mission. The wounded would be brought here from the ship on stretchers and transported back to Chinkiang by truck. Kerans, D-D, Meh and Packard would continue on foot – with a party of stretcher-bearers and an escort of six soldiers supplied by the 177th Regiment. D-D, an Army man accustomed to marching, joked with Kerans about his soft naval feet being unable to take the punishment.

Kerans waited half an hour for the stretcher-bearers to arrive but, anxious that time was against him – and reassured by the 177th Regiment that the Chinese soldiers would know the way to the ship – he decided to press on. To reach the *Amethyst* in her last reported position, off the island of Tai Ping, he had to cross a creek on the river – the Hsiao Ho – at a ferry-point guarded by Nationalist troops. On the map, the four-mile march to the ferry looked easy, but, as they plodded forward along a twisting path with deep ditches on either side, it became apparent that the going would be tough.

Finally, at 9.30pm, the party reached the ferry-point on the west bank of the Hsiao Ho. In the cool dusk they could just make out the shape of junks in the water. They approached the ferryman but couldn't persuade him to take them across the creek. He claimed that the Nationalist guards had just changed the password and, as they had not yet told him the new one, there was a risk he would be fired upon.

The British officers had expected that their expedition to Chinkiang would be a short one, and had therefore brought no food. They now began to feel pangs of hunger. Rummaging in his rucksack, the American doctor found some tins of cheese and a Christmas pudding. This eccentric meal finished, they moved on in a northwesterly direction, following the creek. Only the melancholy bark of mongrels as they passed through villages broke the stillness.

At midnight, after they had been walking for five and a half hours, they heard another sound ahead of them, an English voice: Able Seaman Calcott marched straight up to Lieutenant Commander Kerans and introduced himself. He had been sent ashore from the *Amethyst* in charge of the wounded, he explained, and had already met up with some Chinese stretcher-bearers. The Chinese, it turned out, had stumbled across the ship by chance at its new anchorage in the mouth of the creek, which was about a mile away from its original mooring.

Calcott made his report. The casualties and damage were much more serious than had been first appreciated. Skinner, the ship's captain, had multiple wounds in his shoulder, side and back, and was now dying on a stretcher nearby. He had been among the 16 wounded men who had been landed so far. Weston, the officer who had taken command after Skinner was taken off the ship, was still on board but was himself seriously injured.

Kerans walked the short distance to where the wounded men lay on stretchers. He bent down and spoke to each in turn and then, looking up, he saw the sleek silhouette of HMS *Amethyst* for the first time. She was 100 yards upriver. He decided that Packard and Meh should accompany the wounded back to the assembly-point, while he and D-D should try to get out to the *Amethyst* to bring off the remainder of the wounded and deliver the medical chest. The two officers asked a passing villager if he knew of anyone with a boat. They were directed to a nearby house where they roused an old man and persuaded him to take them over to the *Amethyst*. But, as the old man was working his sweep in the stern of his sampan through the reeds on the bank, it became clear to Kerans that the *Amethyst* was again, for some reason, weighing anchor. 'Bugger me! Look!' he exclaimed to D-D: '*Amethyst* is under way! We're too bloody late!'

The two men stared in disbelief as the *Amethyst* changed her course and moved a little to port. Leaving a trail of smoke across the bows of the sampan, she then glided silently upstream, floating away like a ghost into the darkness. As a last resort, Kerans took out his torch and tried to attract her attention by flashing her in Morse. The frigate gave no answer.

'There is a tide in the affairs of men, which, taken at the flood, leads on to fortune.' John Kerans was about to discover through his own experience the poignancy of Shakespeare's words. For now, though, all he felt was frustration. Switching his flashlight off, he asked the ferryman to take him back to the shore. He and D-D then began the long march back to the assembly-point at Ta Chiang. Two hours later, they found the wounded wrapped in blankets on the roadside. Skinner, the *Amethyst*'s captain, had died. So had an Ordinary Seaman, George Winter, whose face was blown away.

Ten minutes later, reports came through on the radio that the Communists were crossing the Yangtse further downriver, and that the Nationalists were planning to evacuate Chinkiang that night. There was no time to lose. Kerans took the wounded to the station there and got them on the last train to Shanghai, where they could be treated in a properly equipped hospital. He then rang

Donaldson, the Naval Attaché in Nanking, to report on the situation. Donaldson ordered him to get on board HMS *Amethyst* at all costs, to take command, to have the wounded First Lieutenant sent ashore, and to try to take the ship on up to Nanking. D-D was to remain at Chinkiang in case of further difficulties with the wounded.

Kerans turned again to the Chinese Navy for help and, this time, a young sublieutenant volunteered to man a landing-craft for him. By 2pm, on Friday 22 April, he was passing through the narrow, fast and dangerous channel south of Silver Island. Here he looked up and saw an RAF Sunderland flying boat circling overhead. He watched as it landed, presumably alongside the *Amethyst*, and then take off again as the shore batteries fired at it. An hour later, after hugging the south bank, Kerans sighted the *Amethyst*. She had re-anchored in five fathoms, 500 yards from the Nationalist shore. Her decks were deserted. Nonetheless, Kerans came close to being fired upon, because orders had been given that any craft approaching should be covered by the Oerlikons, the small guns mounted on the ship. Luckily, Kerans managed to run to the bows in time. There he stood, waving his open charts flag-wise, and 22-year-old Lieutenant Stuart Hett, one of the few uninjured officers left on board, spotted his uniform through binoculars.

As Kerans came alongside, Hett said, 'Glad to see you, Sir. We have just heard about you.' It was 3pm. The atmosphere was humid. Kerans surveyed the damage. The *Amethyst* had received more than 50 direct hits. Twisted metal and shattered glass littered the whole ship. He was told how 65 ratings had left the vessel in the whaler. Many others never received the order to abandon ship or, if they did, chose to ignore it. There remained onboard some 75 unwounded and, lying in a row, not yet prepared for burial, 17 dead.

Water was swilling the lower decks from burst pipes. The wardroom and all the officers' quarters were uninhabitable. All the heads (latrines) on the ship were blocked. The sick bay was wrecked, and parts of the ship were in darkness. The ship's low power-room was destroyed, her gyro-compass was useless; her electrical, gunnery, lighting and navigational circuits were so damaged that she was unable to steer or defend herself adequately. In accordance with Navy regulations concerning the abandonment of a ship, all radar and other secret equipment had been broken into pieces with mallets and heavy spanners and thrown overboard.

Kerans listened as Hett told him about the man who had died close to Weston, drumming the deck with his heels. He heard how another man had fallen nearby, struck in the artery that passes through the shoulder, a fountain of blood pouring out of him. This had drained out like a river until, in a death convulsion, the man had leapt up, run across the deck and fallen down a hatchway ladder, lifeless.

The coxswain, Chief Petty Officer Rosslyn Nicholls, had been hit by flying shrapnel and grievously wounded in both the right leg and the head. As he had fallen over to his left, he had involuntarily pulled the wheel to port with him. After the shelling had stopped, machine-guns had raked the upper decks. Kerans was told how even men in the water and on life-rafts had been shelled and fired at. As the wounded began to struggle ashore, the small-arms fire had kicked up little spurts of water around them.

For a moment, as the scale of the problem struck him, the new captain of the *Amethyst* felt like an impostor: self-doubt about his own abilities and memories of his uneven record as a commander gnawed away at him. What if, instead of being his finest hour, this adventure ended in him being called once again before a Board of Inquiry? He took a deep breath, squared his shoulders and went to the wireless office in search of the First Lieutenant, Geoffrey Weston. Weston was ashen-faced, breathless and vomiting – but reluctant to leave his post. Kerans ordered him to take the landing-craft back to shore and to meet up with the stretcher-party, which would take him to hospital.

Kerans's second task was to bury the 17 dead; they

were starting to decompose in the heat. It was a harsh way to begin his new command and it must have brought back memories of HMS *Orion*. The bodies were committed to the waters in 12 fathoms, each weighed down with two four-inch shells. Being an Anglican, Kerans read the service for the Protestants, and Petty Officer Stoker Mechanic Jeremiah performed the service for the five Roman Catholics. Volleys of gunfire did not mark their departure, for fear of giving the Communists the wrong signal. The only salute as the bodies passed over the side was the thin pipe of the bo's'n's call.

Next, Kerans called for 'all hands aft' and the ship's company mustered on the quarter-deck. He introduced himself, told them that the wounded had been taken away safely to hospital, and that HMS *Amethyst* would still attempt to reach Nanking, possibly that night.

His priority now was to secure relief for Telegraphist French who had been on continuous duty for two and a half days. He found an electrical mechanic who knew Morse code. By signal to Vice Admiral Sir Alexander Madden, who had ordered the *Amethyst* to sail up the Yangtse in the first place, Kerans then reported his intention to continue the passage to Nanking. To his disappointment, the Admiral replied that he was not to do so that night. Instead the message came: 'The safety of your ship's company being now the first consideration, you are to prepare to evacuate from the ship and sink and march 150 miles to Shanghai. Report when you will be ready.'

Kerans was stupefied. This must be the first time in naval history that an officer had been appointed to command a ship and then immediately ordered to scuttle her, he thought. Then, at midnight, when all were ready to evacuate, they were told that the order to do so would not come that night after all, as the Admiralty had received some hope of diplomatic action – negotiation with the Communists for a safe conduct. Kerans told the ship's company to get some rest.

The next day, Saturday 23 April, dawned silently to a thick fog. The Communists were closing in. All Nationalists troops and naval craft were now abandoning Chinkiang, and road, rail and water traffic was being cut off. When the fog cleared, Kerans caught his first glimpse of Communist troops, their mustard coloured uniforms jostling for space alongside mules on a ragged armada of small Communist junks.

Kerans decided to shift berth a short distance downstream where there was no natural cover for hostile guns. As he was about to anchor, a battery of artillery opened up and he had to turn back at full speed and anchor out of sight of the battery a mile further up. It was the *Amethyst*'s fifth anchorage since getting off the mud on

Rose Island and here she was to remain for the next 100 days, pinned down in a stretch of water a mile wide.

HMS *Amethyst* had become a pawn in a diplomatic war. The New China News Agency issued a hostile statement: 'Public opinion here points out that the British Imperialist Navy had joined hands with Nationalist reactionaries to challenge the People's Liberation Army and directly participated in China's war by firing on PLA positions.' The *Amethyst*, they said, had opened fire first. Kerans suspected that the truth behind the Communists' posturing was that they had realised the enormity of the mistake they had made in opening fire first. In all probability they had mistaken the *Amethyst* for a Nationalist ship – and so they had decided to use the incident for propaganda purposes.

The river was now alive with activity: trading junks, farmers in sampans, great rafts of logs nursed by little tugs, all coming downriver from the inland forests. On the sixth day of the Incident, the weather turned hot and humid and Kerans ordered that everyone onboard should change into white summer rig. There was much to do, he said, rubbing his hands together, trying to keep morale up by making sure his three officers and 72 ratings were busy. 'Lists have to be corrected, leaks repaired and those bloody rats killed,' he told the men with a grin. Simon, the ship's cat who had gone to ground during the shooting, reemerged slightly wounded and went to work.

The Communists, meanwhile, toyed with Kerans – promising that they had sent a messenger to Nanking when they hadn't, being evasive, denying him access to the PLA general in charge of that area. There was one concession they did make, though. The ship was low on fresh food, so Kerans negotiated with the Communist intermediary to arrange for local traders to visit the ship. A sampan manned by three women began making deliveries from the local village. The stores petty officer had to haggle for two hours at a time: working out how much flour and sugar should be bartered for an egg or a pound of potatoes. The traders soon realised they were in a stronger bargaining position and their rates of exchange grew ever more iniquitous. Kerans decided to put the *Amethyst*'s crew on half-rations.

***

The British reaction to the Yangtse Incident was predictable. In London, the Red Flag was burnt. In Dartmouth, Harry Pollitt, leader of the British Communist Party, was booed and chased from a hall when he said the Communists were justified in their actions. At Westminster, on 26 April, Winston Churchill, the leader of the opposition, pressed Clement Attlee, the Prime Minister, to explain what had caused this international crisis on the Yangtse river. 'How is it', the old bruiser growled from his seat opposite the despatch box, 'that at this time we have not got in Chinese waters one aircraft-carrier, if not two, capable of affording protection to our nationals who may be increasingly involved in peril and misfortune, and capable of affording the protection in the only way which is understood by those who are attacking us, murdering us and insulting us, namely, by effective power of retaliation?'

A Government inquiry was set up. This revealed that tension between the Chinese Communists and the supposedly neutral Royal Navy had first begun two years earlier when the Admiralty had agreed plans to lend the Nationalist Chinese Navy some of its ships. Indeed, such was the cosiness of the relationship between the Nationalist government and Sir Ralph Stevenson, the British Ambassador in Nanking, that it had been possible for the British to make a request for their ships to exercise rights of passage along the Yangtse river from Shanghai to Nanking and to station a RN destroyer in the capital. The warship could provide protection for British nationals living and working in the city, Stevenson had argued, and it would afford them moral support and a means of escape at short notice.

The fact that the Communists had made it clear that they would not recognise this agreement had been recklessly ignored by the British. Despite the prevailing air of crisis in the Yangtse region, Vice Admiral Madden, supported by Ambassador Stevenson, had decided to continue with his plan to relieve HMS *Consort* on 20 April. The deadline for the Nationalists to accept the Communists' peace terms had also been 20 April. It was common knowledge that the Nationalists were bound to reject the terms; indeed, they had requested an extension on the deadline for the ceasefire until 25 April, as a delaying tactic. The *Amethyst* had been scheduled to reach Nanking at 3pm, on 20 April, nine hours before the expiry of the ultimatum.

On 30 April the New China News Agency in Peking broadcast a statement drafted by Mao Tse-tung, who seems to have been under the delusion that Churchill was still Prime Minister: 'We denounce the preposterous statement of the warmonger Churchill in the British House of Commons on 26 April,' it read. 'Churchill demanded that the British government should send two aircraft-carriers to the Far East for "effective power of retaliation". What are you retaliating for Mr Churchill? British warships together with Nationalist warships intruded into the defence area of the Chinese People's Liberation Army.'

Meanwhile, back on board the *Amethyst*, two young Communist officers from the shore battery came to see

Kerans. A long and frigid interview revealed that they wanted Kerans to admit that the *Amethyst* had invaded the battlefront of the PLA. Kerans was taken aback and replied that this was a serious political issue which could not possibly be left to an officer of his rank: it should be for the Admiralty and the Ambassador to make such an admission, if, that is, there was a legitimate case for making it. The Chinese disagreed, saying the matter should be settled at a local level.

A few days later, after a two-hour walk on a dusty road, Kerans finally met General Yuan, the short, round PLA commander in the region, at his Chinkiang HQ, a thick-walled, grey stone building festooned in green garlands, Communist propaganda, and a giant blown-up photograph of Mao. Reporters and photographers from the Communist press were waiting to capture the moment that Kerans, and the British Empire he represented, were humiliated.

In the early years of Mao's regime, officers still observed ancient Chinese etiquette. Before the negotiations with Kerans began, therefore, certain formalities had to be observed: each person was given a hot towel and a cup of Chinese tea, and only after the towels had been discarded and the tea drunk did the members of the two delegations shake hands and begin to take up their respective positions on either side of a large, oblong wooden table, the head of which was reserved for General Yuan. Commissar Kang, a humourless man with a cold stare, sat on one side of the long table; Kerans, feeling lonely and isolated, sat on the other. Talking through an interpreter, Yuan presented Kerans with an ultimatum. The Lieutenant Commander was required to plead guilty to invading Communist waters and firing first. He was also to pay compensation for 252 Chinese casualties. Only then would safe passage down the Yangtse be granted to the *Amethyst*.

Kerans, finding it difficult to keep his temper, argued once more that he was not empowered to say these things and that, anyway, they would be lies. He knew that the Communists were sensitive to world opinion so he played on this, saying that, by subjecting his crew to hardship, Yuan was damaging the Communists' name in the world. The meeting broke up acrimoniously.

Over the next few weeks, Kerans had many more meetings with the Communists, 11 in all. Some were with Yuan, but most were with 'Commissar Kang', whom Kerans suspected was really 'Major Kung', the man who had ordered the Communist batteries to fire on the *Amethyst* in the first place.

These negotiations were largely face-saving operations for the Communists. And they were often more about semantic differences than factual ones. The two sides would argue for three hours at a stretch about the meaning of one sentence and even – when it came to replacing 'unfortunately' with the word 'indiscreetly', or 'entering' as opposed to 'intruding' – the definition of one word. The meetings often ended in personal abuse directed at Kerans. Although he was obstinate, Kerans lost his composure only once: he threw his pencil down at one point and told the Commissar's party what he thought of them in plain Anglo-Saxon English.

Some 10,600 miles away, more questions about the incident were being asked in the House of Commons. On one occasion, Harold Macmillan opened the proceedings and, by the time Clement Attlee wound them up six and a quarter hours later, 125 columns of *Hansard* had been filled. Macmillan began that day by describing how the *Amethyst* crisis had unfortunately led to a worsening of Britain's relations with the Communists in China. His theory was that the crisis should never have occurred in the first place. 'I am bound to say that the gunboat mentality seems to be rather out of date.'

He summed up his feelings about the episode with characteristic economy and wit. 'In spite of the agility of the Prime Minister in his statement the other day in skating over some very thin ice, if one takes his story in all its aspects, and takes the responsibilities connected with it, it seems to me that it is an absolute gem, a little cameo of incompetence, a miniature masterpiece of mis-management, a classical illustration, which I have no doubt will long be studied by the staff colleges of the world, of exactly how not to do it.'

The top brass in the Admiralty must have shuddered when they heard these comments – if word got out that their man on the Yangtse hadn't exactly been a model of competence in the past, they would be a laughing-stock. Yet their lack of confidence in John Kerans was misplaced. He was rising to the occasion magnificently.

In eastern China, the rainy season started and, with it, came plagues of cockroaches and mosquitoes. Despite the best efforts of Simon the cat, the ship was now also overrun with rats. Their claws scratched the steel decks all night and their sharp squeals sounded behind the bulkheads. They invaded the mess decks, upper deck and the bridge and ran across men as they slept.

The most pressing consideration for Kerans, though, was not the rats but the shortage of fuel – oil and diesel – which powered the cooling-system engines. Fuel economy had to be introduced; electric power had to be shut down for 12 hours a night. In the heat, without fans, it was stifling. And a stagnant, humid atmosphere built up below decks. As the humidity grew more oppressive, sleep became impossible. Men would try to get some rest on deck but would be driven back below by torrential rain.

During the day, the sun was so hot that the steel on deck burnt the hand. Below deck, the thermometer reached 100 degrees Fahrenheit and the bulkheads steamed with moisture. As if this were not enough, Kerans could see that the men were growing bored, fatigued and unfit. One of them had dysentery. Kerans himself contracted fibrosis brought on by the damp heat of the ship, the humidity on the river, and by the soakings that he got on his visits ashore. Nevertheless life settled into a routine: with a church service every Sunday and a ritual of darkening the port side of the ship every night to avoid temptation to the Communist gunners.

Kerans tried to keep the atmosphere as close to civilised Navy traditions as possible. Every night he dined with his three officers, with a gin and tonic before dinner and a bottle of wine during the meal. Evenings were congenial and good-humoured and the four men would trade jokes about their shipmates. If Kerans was worried, he didn't show it. Indeed, as was remarked upon by his colleagues in the past, he seemed to become calm whenever situations became tense.

One thing really annoyed him, though. There was a pump that discharged over the side of the ship, just near the ladder that he had to use whenever he returned from his meetings with the Communists on shore. He complained about it often to Lieutenant Hett and was always cross when nothing was done to remedy it.

Realising that the best way to avoid melancholy was to keep discipline up and keep the men active so that they would sleep well, Kerans searched for tasks for them to do. He found a trunk of thick mahogany, a delivery for Nanking, and ordered the ratings to saw it up using hand-saws. Hett questioned whether this was really necessary. Friction was beginning to build between the two officers.

Undeterred, Kerans set another seemingly pointless task. He asked Hett to organise the men to bind the anchor cable in bedding from mattresses and grease. He said that squeaking from the chain was keeping him awake at night. But he had another reason for muffling the anchor, one that he wanted to keep from Hett and the other officers for security reasons. Already by this stage he was mulling over the possibility of a breakout at night: a 150-mile dash down the Yangtse to the open sea. He knew that if he was to avoid arousing every Communist artillery battery within a mile, stealth and silence would be essential. To raise the anchor without rattling the heavy chain-cable as it ground through the hawsepipe would be difficult, so he decided instead to slip the cable and leave it in the mud of the Yangtse. To do this a bolt had to be knocked out of one of the half-shackles that joined the lengths of chain together. But even this would mean a short length of cable rattling through the hawsepipe. To avoid a splash as it fell into the water, Kerans decided he would steam slowly up to a point where the cable would be hanging vertically, then release it.

Escape was just a vague consideration at this stage. What the men really needed was reassurance in the form of mail from home. The Communists had been withholding it for two months. Finally, on 20 June, they relented and three bags of mail were delivered to the ship. Even the suspicion that the mail had been tampered with failed to dampen spirits. Kerans was as eager as anyone to see if he had a letter. There was one, from his wife Stephanie written on her favourite 'Capri blue' Dickinson notepaper – the one in which she told him how proud she felt, having heard the news of his new command on the BBC. One can imagine what a balm this affectionate letter must have been to John Kerans's nerves. In the four years of their marriage, he and Stephanie had spent just four months together. He hadn't seen her – or his daughter – since 1947. And it must have been inspiring for him to learn that the world's press was following his every move.

The conditions on board were getting worse, though, and the strain was beginning to show on his men. Lack of disinfectant, DDT, penicillin and ethyl chloride was making life intolerable. The rats had now made the after part of the ship uninhabitable. On 22 June Kerans had to steel himself to take another drastic step: he shut down all power for periods of two and a half days at a stretch.

Kerans explained to General Yuan just how critical the situation had become. The Royal Navy had a reserve of oil drums for emergencies outside Nanking, he added, and these could be sent downriver. After a week, Yuan granted this request. A tug arrived. The men all stripped to the waist and loaded the 294 drums (54 tons) by hand, working for 11 hours.

As the official code-books had been destroyed at Rose Island and the Communists were probably reading any messages sent from the ship, Kerans had to hint in a signal to the Commander-in-Chief Far East Station, Admiral Sir Patrick Brind – or 'Daddy' Brind, as he was known – that he might try to escape. So as not to alert the Communists, he said that he would try to move the *Amethyst* if there was a 'typhoon'. He hoped the Admiral would understand what this meant. Brind replied cryptically. Buried among some bland thoughts about the typhoon season were the lines, 'The golden rule of making an offing and taking plenty of sea room applies particularly... I shall of course support your judgment.' After much agonising, Kerans interpreted Brind's signal as being permission to break out, at his discretion.

Admiral Brind and Kerans, a trained cipher officer, then worked out between them a new code borrowed from the Germans. It used the first Christian name of the next of kin of all the British naval officers and ratings on board, in alphabetical order. These letters were translated into groups of figures. The system nearly broke down when one young rating could not remember his mother's Christian name: he used to call her 'Bastard'.

Commissar Kang started using delaying tactics, postponing meetings with Kerans. Worried on Kerans's behalf, 'Daddy' Brind sent a signal to Donaldson, the Naval Attaché in Nanking: 'I think this is another trick on Kerans and feel he is nearing the end of his tether, the Communists know it and are playing with him. It seems that you should go to the *Amethyst* to bring matters to a head and complete present negotiations.' In Brind's opinion, the Communists were opposed to Donaldson conducting the talks because he would be fresh, unlike Kerans who was far from well and under extreme pressure.

The Admiralty, realising the strain Kerans was under, and knowing how unstable he had been in the past, gave instructions to Brind to go over the head of General Yuan and secure an interview with Mao Tse-tung, to resolve the dispute once and for all at the highest level. This showed how ignorant the Admiralty was in its dealings with the Communists. The era of the Raj was over. Britannia no longer ruled the waves. 'Daddy' Brind was in no position to demand an interview with anyone, least of all Mao.

The final meeting between Kerans and Kang was on 23 July. The atmosphere was charged. Kang insulted the Lieutenant Commander for 40 minutes, calling him, among other things, a wretched failure. In turn, Kerans became a little paranoid and wondered if, somehow, the Chinese had got hold of information about his past record as a naval officer. Negotiations continued for four hours but no compromise was reached and it was made clear to the stoical Kerans that the *Amethyst* was still a hostage and, unless he made a false confession of guilt, she would remain so.

Admiral 'Daddy' Brind, sensing that Kerans was at breaking-point, sent a message to the by now foul-smelling, disease-ridden *Amethyst*: 'It is clear that the Communists have been holding you hostage to wring admissions from the British government which would not only be untrue and dishonourable but would harm the cause of free nations in the future... For the present, therefore, you are in the forefront of what is now being called the Cold War. I know it is a pretty hot war as far as you are concerned and your stand is widely recognised and greatly admired.'

Four days later, when the temperature on board the floating prison reached 110 degrees in the engine-room and 128 degrees in the boiler-room, Brind sent another morale-boosting message: 'No one can say how this will end, but of one thing I am quite sure, neither the British government, the *Amethyst*'s ship's company nor myself will ever submit to threats, insults and perversions of the truth; nor shall we do anything to harm our country's honour.'

Even though John Kerans was a practical man, rather than an idealist or an historical romantic, his sinews were stiffened by this signal. 'British spirit in adversity has once again shown itself to be unassailable,' he replied to Brind. And at 3pm, on Saturday 30 July 1949, the 101st day of the ship's captivity, he decided that the time had come to attempt a high-speed, 150-mile escape to the open sea.

***

At the time the Lieutenant Commander was making his decision, he was standing on the bridge, smoking a cigarette, wearing nothing but sandals and sunglasses and a towel around his waist. But he knew it was not a resolution to be taken lightly: at stake were his ship and 72 lives as well as his country's honour. It was unlikely that a court martial would be impressed by talk of wresting the initiative from the enemy if his escape-bid ended in disaster. He put his odds of covering the 150 miles to the open sea – running a gauntlet of enemy guns, with half a crew, in a shell-damaged ship, in the dark, over hazardous waters, without lights, pilot, adequate charts, compass, secure codes for signals, gyro or radar – at no more than 50/50.

Yet, once he had made up his mind, he felt calm and in command of the situation. He reached the fo'c'sle, sat down on a bollard on the port side, lit another cigarette and looked out over the brown, rushing floodwaters of the Yangtse to the hazy riverbank beyond.

He told himself he had no real alternative. If he waited another day, the ship would have to go on to quarter food rations. And the fuel situation was critical; by the following afternoon there wouldn't be enough to make it to the open sea. Above all, the moon that night would be at its darkest and therefore most favourable; there had been a new moon on 25 July and tonight the young moon would set at one minute past 11pm. After this, the hours of darkness would shorten and, for the following four weeks, it would be bright, which would make the ship an easier target for the shore batteries.

But 11pm was too late to give him time to complete the long passage to the sea under cover of darkness – first light next morning would be 5.30am – he would therefore have to leave at 10pm. By taking the risk of starting an hour earlier he would give himself seven hours to cover the 150 miles, at a speed of 20 knots, which he thought he could manage with the help of the swift-flowing current.

He examined the Chinese chart that would help him

from Rose Island onwards, but he knew that for the 14-mile stretch to the island he would have no navigational charts at all. There would be guns all the way to Shanghai, he guessed, especially guarding the boom at Kiang Yin, a wide stretch of the river; and, as this boom wasn't a conventional floating barrier but a line of old ships that had been sunk with only a narrow channel between them, it was going to be particularly hazardous. The most formidable challenge, though, would be the six-inch coast-defence guns with their searchlights at the Woo Sung and Pao Shan forts at the mouth of the Yangtse.

At 6.30pm, Kerans summoned the engine-room artificer to his cabin to break the news – in order to give him enough time to raise steam, as well as to make arrangements for producing black smoke, to help conceal the ship when she came under fire. At 7.45pm, he called his 17 chief and petty officers to his cabin. 'I have decided', he said simply, 'to break out tonight at 2200. The risks will be high but I calculate that, if we all pull together, we can bloody well make it.' Everyone was electrified, although Hett, his second-in-command, felt miffed that Kerans hadn't discussed his plans for escape with him earlier. Hett felt the maverick Kerans lacked that elusive thing 'Term Spirit'.

'If we come under fire,' Kerans continued after a pause, 'guns are not to reply unless ordered, because this will enable the shore batteries to lay more accurately. If the ship should be badly hit I will beach her, evacuate her and blow her up myself. The ship's company, by whatever means available, will try to get to Shanghai.'

Kerans explained his plan for silently slipping the grease- and bedding-covered cables. He then ordered all white paint to be blackened and for grease to be smeared over the shining brasswork of the sirens. No white clothing was to be worn on the upper deck, he ordered.

By now pumped up with adrenaline, the captain of the *Amethyst* turned to his next task: to disguise the shape of the ship by altering its silhouette to resemble one of the Chinese landing-craft that had been passing up and down the river. To do this, he rigged black canvas screens from the area to the rear of the bridge and funnel forward to 'A gun' and then on to the extreme point of the bows. (The ship's main armament was six four-inch guns mounted in pairs behind armoured shields; two pairs of these twin guns, A and B, were mounted forward of the bridge.) Kerans then set up green-over-red yardarm lights which he had observed civilian shipping using in the area.

For the next half-hour, the ship's company worked frantically, their excitement palpable. Then, for a moment, it seemed it might all end before it had begun. At the height of the preparation – 8.25pm – the ship's regular Chinese vegetable traders approached in a small sampan.

There was a stunned silence as everyone weighed up the same possibility: the traders might tip off the gun batteries on shore as to what was going on onboard the ship. As ever, Kerans kept his head and ordered his men to stop whatever it was they were doing and bring camp-beds and hammocks on to the deck. He told some of the men to get undressed and pretend to be asleep on the beds, while others were to head off the traders and complain loudly that the Chinese had only brought half the goods they were supposed to, adding that they would have to return next day. It worked.

Ammunition was brought up for B gun; the sick bay was made ready for casualties; lifebelts and helmets were put on. At 9pm, Kerans, wearing a khaki shirt and grey flannels, went on the bridge to accustom his eyes to the night-time gloom. His mouth had gone dry but, when he examined his hands for nerves, they were steady.

Using his new code, Kerans signalled Brind, who was hosting a dinner onboard HMS *Belfast* in Hong Kong. His message read simply that he was planning to escape that night. 'Daddy' Brind received a second signal, from the Admiralty. It said that under no circumstances was Kerans to attempt a break-out without authorisation from London. Brind turned a Nelson's blind eye to it, sending the signal back to the Admiralty for rechecking. Just before 10pm, Brind rapped the dinner-table and said:

'Ladies and gentlemen, a toast to the *Amethyst*.'

The ship, waking from a long sleep, began to hum and pulse. At every voice-pipe, ears were pricked, waiting for the captain's order to go. Kerans checked his watch and, as the minutes ticked towards ten, he scanned the pale moon. A cloud was scudding towards it. He waited a few minutes more.

Ahead, the silence was broken by the distant mutter of an engine. From the bridge, Kerans saw a fully-lit merchant ship, the *Kiang Ling Liberation*, rounding the bend of Ta Sha Island on its way downriver. He realised this was not so much a danger as an opportunity. The ship could act as pilot for the most difficult part of *Amethyst*'s passage, the 14 miles to Rose Island, for which he had no chart. Kerans would follow astern of her. Picking up the telephone, he gave the order to the wheelhouse: 'Ring on main engines. Obey telegraphs. 180 revolutions.'

A few minutes later, after the ship had left her berth and executed a 180-degree turn, he added: 'Slow ahead, port. Midships.' The ship began to glide ahead. At 10.12pm Kerans rang the fo'c'sle party and gave the order: 'Slip.' As Kerans had calculated, the muffled cable didn't make a sound as it was dropped vertically into the water. It was a symbolic act, the hostage ship breaking free of her chains. 'Wheel hard a-starboard,' Kerans ordered through the wheelhouse voice-pipe. 'Starboard engine half astern.

Port engine half ahead.' The *Amethyst*'s bows swung off sharply, 45 degrees to starboard. As they did so, a fountain of sparks flew out of the funnel, sending Kerans's heart racing. The damaged brickwork of No 1 boiler was the cause. No one on shore seemed to notice, though. No flare came. 'Stop starboard,' Kerans said. 'Half ahead both engines. Midships.' The *Amethyst* was underway.

For 30 minutes, she pursued her silent, shadowy course, checking the echo soundings all the way. Then, as she passed Ta Chiang at 10.30pm, a flare shot into the sky ahead of the merchant ship, challenging her. When the *Kiang Ling Liberation* replied with the usual siren signals and altered course a little to starboard, the *Amethyst* followed her. At the same time, Kerans noticed another small vessel on his port bow, again fully lit. It was a landing-craft. A second flare went up and, this time, the *Amethyst* was illuminated. Then the landing-craft let go a burst of machine-gun fire across her bows, a challenge for the *Amethyst* to heave to. Kerans prepared to ram. But then he realised that, in the confusion, the craft was directing its fire at the shore battery. The artillery on shore retaliated and *Amethyst* was under heavy assault, from both banks, caught in a crossfire of field guns and semi-automatics. 'Full ahead both engines,' Kerans ordered. He then altered course 15 degrees to port and called for black smoke.

A wild and confused fight followed, with shells, orange flashes and red tracer bullets spitting in all directions. The *Amethyst* was hit on the starboard waterline. She shook and heeled over violently. Water poured in but the hole was plugged and the pumps put to work. Kerans ordered B gun to open fire but, because of the heavy list, it couldn't. Only the Oerlikon and Bren guns were able to come into action. The captain sent a signal to Admiral Brind at 10.33pm: 'Am under heavy fire and have been hit.'

Kerans now began a struggle to right the ship by weaving from port to starboard, but steering was difficult and soon he ran into shallow water. Then, almost as suddenly as she had heeled over, the ship righted herself and B gun was able to open fire. The *Amethyst* worked up to full steam and, throwing great bow waves which spread out to break upon the shores, plunged past the *Kiang Ling Liberation* with 18 inches to spare amid a cloud of her own dense smoke. When Kerans looked back, he saw that the 600-ton Chinese steamer had been hit by her own side.

The enemy was now fully alerted, sending word on ahead. But Kerans went for maximum speed through the swirling waters, negotiating shifting sandbanks in the dark. Whenever the Communists got their artillery batteries in position to fire, the ship had already raced past them. A report reached the bridge that water was flooding rapidly through the old wound in the tiller flat. It was kept under control, with the watertight doors shut, by two young hands who knew that if the worst occurred they stood no chance of survival.

Just before 1am, the frigate closed on her next danger-point: the boom at Kiang Yin. As she approached, she was again challenged by flares from the shore and, when her identity was realised, she came under fire again, not only from the shore but also from a nearby ship. Her speed and her black smoke had baffled the shore gunners and, in a few minutes, she was astern of their line of fire. A moment of dangerous uncertainty now faced Kerans. Unless the boom was closed altogether, he would expect to see two lighted buoys ahead, marking either side of the safe channel. The captain saw only one. Which side of this light should he try? If he chose wrongly, the escape-bid would end explosively, the bottom of the vessel would be ripped open and she would sink, joining the other sunken wrecks littering the river-bed. He decided the least risk was to pass as close to the buoy as possible. 'Port 10,' he said into the voice-pipe. 'Ease to five... midships... steer 062 degrees.' He held his breath.

There was no sickening impact and the shell-scarred *Amethyst* made it through the boom. Half an hour later, Kerans was able to signal to 'Daddy' Brind: 'Halfway.' At 2.45am, having completed 100 sea miles of his passage, he sent another: 'Hundred up.' Brind replied with a line worthy of a *Boy's Own* comic: 'A magnificent century!'

By now, after nearly five hours on the run, the tension was taking its toll on the *Amethyst*'s crew: the lookouts on the bridge were drooping with fatigue; those in the engine-room were dripping with sweat; in the boiler-room the temperature had reached 170 degrees and two men had fainted.

The last hurdle was approaching: the forts at Pao Shan and Woo Sung, armed with their powerful six-inch guns. Just one hit from one of those guns on the waterline would be enough to sink the *Amethyst*. There was little chance that their searchlights would miss them. At 5am, Kerans could see the white fingers of light searching the dark water ahead, sweeping methodically across the area through which the ships would have to pass. He ordered the engine-room to give him everything they had got. As the ship came nearer, one of the beams of light swung towards them and momentarily the ship was suffused. But it passed over them and no guns opened up. The cold light swept over them a second time. Again no guns blazed. Eventually, the light was astern of the frigate.

Ten minutes later, Kerans got his first glimpse of daylight and, at 29 minutes past five, within a minute of the time he had calculated for the journey, the distant outline of HMS *Concord*, a destroyer, could be seen. Rodney, the captain of the *Concord*, was an old friend of

Kerans. 'Fancy meeting you again', he signalled. Kerans replied with feeling: 'Never, never has a ship been more welcome.' The scarred and rusty Royal Navy frigate was out in the open sea again after 101 days of captivity. The saltwater lapped her hull once more and the sea breeze filled the lungs of her crew. Kerans checked the ship's fuel. Incredibly, she was down to just nine tons, which effectively meant she was running on empty.

HMS *Concord* came alongside and all her company went on deck to cheer. Many of the men onboard the *Amethyst* were crying with relief. Those in the boiler-room collapsed from exhaustion – they had had to drink close to a gallon of tea each to stop from dehydrating in the extreme temperatures down below. Kerans looked pale and drawn but felt elated. He knew that, as a feat of nerve, daring and seamanship, what he had just pulled off was unique in naval history.

Stuart Hett, the First Lieutenant, who was on the point of collapse having navigated on the bridge for the past seven and a half hours, now asked Kerans if he had a last signal he would like to send to Admiral Brind in Hong Kong. Kerans thought for a moment. He wanted to say something with enough weight and significance to do justice to the moment. 'Yes,' he said, 'take this down. "Have rejoined the Fleet south of Woo Sung. No damage or casualties. God save the King." '

***

As soon as he heard the news of the *Amethyst*'s escape, King George VI took the unusual step of awarding an immediate DSO to her captain, Lieutenant Commander John Kerans. The King also sent a telegram to the C-in-C of the Far East Station, Admiral Brind. It read: 'Please convey to the commanding officer and ship's company of HMS *Amethyst* my hearty congratulations on their daring exploit to rejoin the Fleet. The courage, skill and determination shown by all onboard have my highest commendation. Splice the mainbrace.'

The Admiral passed the message on to Kerans as, refuelled and escorted by other Royal Navy ships, the frigate was approaching Hong Kong. He added a note of warning: 'What you have gone through in the Yangtse is child's play to the publicity you are going to face.'

He was right. Kerans achieved instant fame. His dramatic adventure was hailed in the West as a triumph of the human spirit; and, as far as the Admiralty was concerned, all his past sins were forgiven and forgotten – or, rather, hastily covered up. They could see the propaganda value in hailing Kerans as the latest in a long line of swashbuckling British Empire heroes, from Drake and Raleigh to Nelson.

The emergence of a new folk hero could not have come

at a better time for Attlee's government. The Great Britain of 1949 was, after all, a gloomy place. Austerity even exceeded wartime levels as the bankrupt country lacked the foreign currency to buy the food needed from abroad. The pound had just been devalued by 30%, from a value of $4 to $2.8. The nation was plagued by strikes; with the dockers in particular crippling the economy. Rationing was still in force. And, perhaps the biggest blow to national pride, since India had been given independence two years earlier, the sun was finally setting on the British Empire. With the Iron Curtain going up, the testing of the first Soviet atom bomb, and the Berlin Airlift, which had begun the previous year and continued until the spring of 1949, the Cold War had started in earnest.

In other words, it was hardly surprising that Kerans's escape provided a boost for national morale out of proportion to its military significance. His breakout – as well as his stirring signal about the King – made headlines all over the world. Everywhere, that is, except in China. It was only after two days of silence, in which the Yangtse was closed to all traffic, that the inevitable condemnation from the Communists came. The airwaves exploded with cries for retribution; the presses rattled off stories about how the British imperialists had blood on their hands. Chinese newspapers claimed the *Kiang Ling Liberation* had been used as a shield by Kerans and then deliberately hit by him, leading to the deaths of hundreds of passengers. Not content with stealing away from the scene of the crime, the *Amethyst* was alleged to have deliberately fired upon the lifeboats that had come out to rescue the survivors, 'an act of calculated wickedness'.

These claims were easy to dismiss, not least because the captain of the Chinese merchant ship had given an interview to the Press Association before the Communist authorities had got to him – and in it he explained that the PLA had sunk his ship, not the British, and that 40 Chinese lives had been lost, not hundreds. The firing had continued for 15 minutes after the *Amethyst* left the scene, he said. Besides, there was no logic in the British sinking their own shield.

At first, Attlee's government didn't think it expedient to sound too triumphant about the escape. The summer of 1949 was a delicate time in Sino-British relations, not least because the British had clearly backed the wrong horse in the Chinese civil war. (Although Britain claimed to be neutral, its support for the Nationalists had been implicit.) Mao's victorious army had come to a halt just 25 miles away from Hong Kong. And, according to records that were released 50 years later, Attlee had secretly been prepared to hand the British colony over to the Chinese leader, had he demanded it.

But once the Chinese Communists stepped up their

campaign of abuse against the British – saying among other things that the imperialists were 'shameless, vicious hypocrites who would have to pay for their crimes in blood' – and, once they had made accusations that could not go unanswered, Attlee felt the world had to be told the English version of the truth concerning the Yangtse Incident. If he did not refute the Chinese interpretation, it might soon take on a cloak of respectability in the eyes of other nations.

The British gloves came off and the celebrations began. Despite torrential rain, hundreds of craft met the battered frigate outside Hong Kong harbour on 3 August and, with sirens sounding, they accompanied her to her berth. Spitfires flew overhead and dipped their wings in salute. A fusillade of firecrackers began all over the colony, the smoke from them so thick in places the traffic had to be stopped. At the quayside to receive her were thousands of people, among them the Governor of Hong Kong, the C-in-C of the Far East Station, and an army of photographers and reporters.

A hail of telegrams arrived onboard the ship from sources as diverse as the British Housewives' League and the British Jewellery Trade. Even Simon the ship's cat received some, the usual message being: 'Heartiest Purrs!' Kerans pinned up most of the pink-coloured 'Imperial Telegrams' on the bridge, so that the men could read them. One, from the White Ensign Club in Cape Town, read: 'Neither galleons, U-boats nor Iron Curtain, nor piracy, blackmail or ransom assail thee o valiant *Amethyst*. Thy kinsmen send thee greetings, true descendant of Drake and faithful servant of the King.'

Billy Whistler, aged nine, wrote: 'How proud it makes me feel to know that such brave men are guarding our seas... Now we can hold our heads up again as we haven't been able to do for three years...'

There was a revealing cable, addressed to Kerans, from his cousin Harold: 'I was giving up hope, being a pessimist, but I should have realised the supplies of gin would be getting low and it would take all the devils of Hell to stand between you and fresh supplies. It's been the only good news we've had in three years and this government should be grateful to you for getting it out of a hole and saving face in China. You should be a made man. However, if you never become Admiral, you have certainly written a page in the history of the Royal Navy.'

Feeling slightly overwhelmed by the response, John Kerans was ushered towards a BBC microphone for a rather stilted conversation with his wife Stephanie, who was waiting in a studio in Bush House, London. It was the first time the couple had spoken in 18 months. Since the escape, Stephanie had been inundated with requests for interviews from the press. At one stage she had had to hold an impromptu press conference in her small sitting-room, for the benefit of dozens of reporters. She didn't mention this ordeal in her broadcast.

John: (in a clipped, BBC World Service voice): Have you heard I'm bringing the *Amethyst* home?

Stephanie: (after a delay): That's wonderful.

John: I'm afraid I lost all my gear in Nanking.

Stephanie: Is there any chance of getting it sent overland?

John: I'm afraid not. Not with my name on it. It will never get through. Don't worry, I haven't lost the cigarette case.

A more relaxed and insightful letter from Stephanie arrived a few days later, written from 19 St Flora's Road, Littlehampton, and dated 6 August 1949:

'My own darling John,

'Words just can't express what I'm feeling: I'm so very, very proud of you, darling – no wife was ever more proud of a husband and no DSO was ever more thoroughly deserved. As no doubt you are fully aware, this amazing escape, successful to the nth degree, yet with all the odds so apparently against it, has had the most wonderful effect in uplifting every soul in this country and all over the world (at least, where Communism is not accepted!) at a time when there really doesn't appear to be a great deal of light on the horizon. It's almost like a fantastic fairy-tale.

'A week ago, at 2159, I was not feeling particularly happy with life: then, in the space of a minute, my whole outlook was changed. I very nearly shot out of my skin when the 10 o'clock news started with: "HMS *Amethyst* has slipped her moorings... etc." I was so terribly excited. Somehow, I had not thought that you wouldn't be successful, but oh! the joy and relief to hear an hour later, your now famous signal: "Have rejoined the Fleet..." I just had to kneel down and thank God. I cried a little bit, too. To think that after all those weeks it was over at last. What relief you must have felt. I feel your last month in that damned river must have been ghastly and beyond imagination...

'It was uncanny and quite incredible speaking to you yesterday morning and oh what an hour! – 0745 here. It needed quite a bit of engineering for me to get to the BBC, as you may have imagined. Having packed Charmian and torn up to Joy's on Wednesday night, I got up to the BBC by 0700. They broadcast a bit of our conversation on the news last night – went over very well. Incidentally, I gather you intended me to realise which cigarette case you'd managed to hang on to!! What a hopeless tease you are! The funniest thing is that the *Daily Telegraph*, referring to our conversation, indicates that it must have been a present from me!! Is your girlfriend Ann still in this country, incidentally, or has she gone back to America?

'I thought, possibly, your kit might have been sent overland to Hong Kong when you first joined *Amethyst*. I quite agree, if it's still there, the thugs are not very likely to hand it over to Lieutenant Commander Kerans, DSO. What a damn shame – that'll be the third time, won't it? One thing I'm pleased about – I feel sure you won't be going back to Hong Kong. As you know, it's always rankled that I've never been with you, but somehow I feel that from now things might really be different. Perhaps our fourth wedding anniversary will mark the beginning of our married life. I hope you want it as much as I do, darling. Also, it's high time Charmian had a father!

'Queen Mary's Lady in Waiting wrote to me. Queen Mary was deeply touched by your final sentence: "God save the King." All letters, telegrams and newspapers I'm keeping so there'll be more for you to see when you return...

'Am already on the lookout for another house and hope to settle on one before the 23rd and move in about mid-October. In the meantime, I'll go home to Tavistock to save a few pennies. Mrs Kerans will need to have some new and very nice clothes for when the Commander comes home and, at the price things are, I can visualise no change out of £50. Better let me have some pay that's been accumulating, darling!

'Again, darling, congratulations and undying admiration for a really brilliant piece of work. From your proud and loving wife Stephanie.

'PS British Movietone News took Charmian and me – so you may see it out there before you see us!

'PPS Sorry this is a PS but do take care of yourself and get that rheumatism better.'

History does not relate who the mysterious 'Ann' was or how Kerans had come to lose his kit on the previous two occasions. The reference to rheumatism is telling, though. On the *Amethyst*'s 10,600-mile journey home to England, Kerans also suffered from malaria, jaundice and flu. His condition was not helped by the constant celebrations that marked the voyage. At Singapore, Penang, Colombo, Aden, Fayid, Port Said, Malta and Gibraltar, the ship was welcomed with cheering crowds, assembled bands, parades, banquets, bunting, gun salutes, fireworks and cocktail parties. Where once Kerans had drunk to forget, now he drank to celebrate and, at nearly every port of call, he had to be helped from the bars and night-clubs. Back on the bridge, his spirits were high and he engaged in constant banter with his new First Lieutenant, Peter Berger, who had been wounded and taken to hospital after navigating the *Amethyst* on her initial journey up the Yangtse. The two men hit it off and Berger (who was later knighted and promoted to Vice-Admiral) found the now confident Kerans charming and likeable.

Such was the build-up of excitement as the *Amethyst*

neared home that one newspaper ran the headline: '*Amethyst*: only 10 days to go!' As the English coastline came into view, Kerans blew it a kiss. He ordered that the tattered White Ensign that had been flown throughout the months of the ship's captivity should now be taken out of the cupboard and hoisted once more at the stern for the benefit of the cameras.

At dawn on 1 November, with the ship's company lined up on deck, shivering in the keen southeast wind, the *Amethyst*'s sleek grey outline sailed up Plymouth Sound, nosed her way through the water of Devonport harbour and docked at Plymouth Hoe. A Lancaster flew overhead and dipped its wings in salute and there were scenes of euphoria to eclipse even those witnessed in Hong Kong. Thousands of well-wishers lined the quayside, their handkerchiefs fluttering. John Kerans scanned the crowd for the first sight of his wife and daughter. Stephanie, wearing a dark overcoat, and Charmian, carrying her favourite sailor doll, made their way down the gangplank, through a crush of microphones and popping flash-bulbs. Stephanie kissed her husband and said: 'I hope you're going to stay in the country this time!' The cameras clicked. Kerans turned to them and said: 'I'll try, darling. It's good to be back. But I'm fiendishly cold.' The crowd laughed warmly.

Three VIPs – Viscount Hall, the First Lord of the

Admiralty, Lord Fraser, the First Sea Lord, and Admiral Sir Robert Burnett, the Commander-in-Chief, Plymouth – were at Devonport to greet the returning hero. The thin notes of the bo's'n's pipe as the VIPs came aboard could hardly be heard above the cheering and the siren blasts from the other ships in the harbour. Once ashore, the ship's company, led by the band of the Royal Marines, marched for a mile to Royal Parade. The crowds lining the route were 20 deep. Men waved union flags, women threw paper streamers. Many had waited for three hours. The crew filed into a hotel for a civic luncheon at which Drake's drum was on display. the *Daily Telegraph*, the *Illustrated London News*, the *Daily Graphic* and the *Sunday Empire News* had all brought out special souvenir supplements to commemorate the event. A cartoon in the *Daily Express* showed Trafalgar Square without Nelson on top of his column. The caption read: 'Gone to meet the *Amethyst*.'

The next parade for the ship's company in London was an even grander affair. Kerans warned his crew to look after their cap-bands as they had become prized souvenirs for young women. 'And don't mix your drinks afterwards,' he added with a smile. 'Because I don't want to have to come down to Bow Street to bail you buggers out!'

In a thick fog, the ship's company – this time joined by the men of HMS *Consort, Black Swan* and *London* as well as the crew of the Sunderland flying boat – were inspected by Clement Attlee and Lord Hall at Horse Guards Parade before they marched up Whitehall to Trafalgar Square for a service of thanksgiving in St Martin-in-the-Fields. Traffic in the area was held up from 11.20am until 1pm, as the column then marched to the Guildhall for a reception by the Lord Mayor. After dining on casserole of roast chicken, the Prime Minister made a speech and this was followed by one from Kerans in which he stressed that the escape had been a team effort, not just his doing. 'I was one of the few commanders who, 24 hours after taking control, was told to sink his ship!' This anecdote was becoming his party piece.

The following day, officers and their relatives went to Buckingham Palace for a special investiture in the white and gold state ballroom. Afterwards, as all sipped sherry, John Kerans was introduced to the princesses, and the King, dressed in the uniform of an Admiral of the Fleet, presented Stephanie Kerans with a watercolour miniature of the *Amethyst*. That evening, the *News of the World* hosted a dinner in the ship's honour at the Dorchester. There were 500 guests and Mrs Kerans cut the iced cake, which was made in the shape of a frigate.

Whether he wanted to be or not, Kerans had become one of the first real celebrities of the media age. Indeed, it would hardly be an exaggeration to say that the country was in the grip of Kerans-mania. People were naming their babies 'Kerans'. The 'Kerans cocktail' became the rage ($1/4$ gin; $1/4$ Crème de Noyaux; $1/4$ Grand Marnier; $1/4$ orange cordial and a dash of Angostura bitters). At a National Book Exhibition he was mobbed by young women wanting his autograph. He was asked to do after-dinner speeches as well as open fêtes and even, on one occasion, an old people's home.

Did the fame go to his head? Perhaps a little, though Kerans was always a rather nonchalant character, and he floated on the applause with log-like calm. If anything, being naturally shy and reserved, he found his treatment embarrassing. He wasn't alone in finding the prolonged emotionalism a bit over the top. One disgruntled RN commander wrote to the *Times*: 'The hysteria so easily worked up about HMS *Amethyst* is another symptom of the unhealthy state of public opinion. It was reminiscent of the bobbysoxers crowding a Waterloo platform to acclaim an arriving transatlantic film star.'

Elsewhere in the Senior Service, there was resentment about the fuss being made of the Yangtse Incident so soon after the war. Naval officers who had had to endure much worse in the Atlantic convoys felt that what amounted to an undignified retreat for the *Amethyst* shouldn't be glorified. And, after the initial euphoria died down, there were even murmurings about Kerans. Some of the ship's company felt he was stealing the limelight. Lieutenant Hett, for example, felt he wasn't given the credit he deserved for navigating the ship down the Yangtse (everyone assumed it was Kerans who had done the navigation and, according to Hett, he had done nothing to discourage this view).

A month after the *Amethyst*'s return, a leaked memo revealed that the First Sea Lord in London and the British Ambassador in Nanking had initially been aghast that Kerans had so cavalierly taken matters into his own hands on the Yangtse, without consulting higher authority in advance. And after news reached them that the escape had been a success, they admitted to astonishment that this complex and rebellious man had proved himself to be such an inspirational leader during a crisis. Far from being reckless or unreliable, they acknowledged, Kerans had shown remarkable resolve and restraint in his frustrating negotiations with the Communists, and great skills of seamanship in getting his ship down the Yangtse.

At the same time, Vice Admiral Madden must have been conscious of the fact that his own role in the whole affair had not been beyond criticism: in agreeing to Ambassador Stevenson's request to relieve the guardship at Nanking, he had taken an unnecessary risk. At best, sending the *Amethyst* up the Yangtse at the height of the civil war had been a provocative act. At worst, it had been an embarrassing blunder. Kerans had saved Madden's, and the Admiralty's, face. And the fact that the men of the *Amethyst* felt they owed their lives to Kerans's charisma, flair and courage could not be ignored. On 31 December 1949, it was decided at the Admiralty that Kerans should be rewarded with promotion to Commander. A few in the Royal Navy bristled at this, arguing that, while he deserved his DSO, promotion would be at someone else's expense. But most applauded the decision.

***

For two years, from early 1950, Commander John Kerans, DSO worked for naval intelligence at the Admiralty in London. As he was still being lionised as a national hero – giving talks, collaborating on a book about the Yangtse Incident – it was an agreeable time for him, but he hankered for the sea. His wishes came true in December 1952, when he was given command of the minesweeper, HMS *Rinaldo*.

Ill-health made his happiness short-lived. 'My darling Stephanie', he wrote from the ship on 21 January 1953. 'Afraid I'm in a somewhat depressed frame of mind with a stomach that refuses to mend itself. Influenzal gastritis they call it... What has happened in the ship, I don't know. I did ask the MO who came on at Spithead to ring you. I hope he did – I gave him half a crown. Your thoroughly depressed but ever loving husband, John.'

John Kerans had never been much of a letter-writer but now, prompted by loneliness, he began writing several long letters a week to Stephanie. Sometimes these were gossipy in tone: 'My Darling Stephanie, yes, I had a very short w/e with Sam Hadow... Quite a nice little wife...' Often the letters concerned mundane domestic details: 'Darling S, I shall increase your allotment this month to £35. I agree, go for the Hoover. At present a second bed is not a dire necessity...'

It was while on the bridge of the *Rinaldo* that he heard of the birth of his second daughter, on 18 June 1953. 'My darling S, congratulations. Well done', he wrote to his wife. 'Am still sceptical about calling her Melanie Amethyst Kerans but am prepared to pander to female wishes for once... 8lbs seems a whopper! Hope it wasn't too painful an extraction. I think after this we tie a knot in it... I spoke to Miss K senior, whose reaction seemed somewhat negative.'

There was speculation in the press that Kerans would name his second daughter Amethyst. In the end, the name on the birth certificate was Melanie June Kerans.

Stephanie Kerans put a brave face on being apart from the father of her young children. 'I believe the best years of my life are occurring now,' she said in an interview. 'Fame was ours but fame is costly – though there are some who mistakenly believe it goes hand in hand with wealth. Service life is of necessity expensive, with its upheavals and removals – from one furnished house to the next... Yet there is a zest in this uncertain life and excitement in wondering what is around the corner – not knowing what fate has in store – that makes these years so happy.'

For one year, from 1954 to 1955, Stephanie finally got the chance to join the Commander on a posting abroad. The couple were based in Bangkok, though Stephanie was often still on her own because John's new job – he was the British Naval Attaché there – meant he also had to cover Phnom Penh, Vientiane, Saigon and Rangoon. And he was flying constantly between these cities.

'His reputation was not good in the Far East,' according to Commander David Hunter who worked with Kerans in Bangkok. 'In fact, it used to be said that Kerans was famous for two things: he had the biggest balls in the Royal Navy and he was the stupidest officer in the Royal Navy. I cannot vouch for one of these accolades but I did encounter him professionally when the second did not seem too unlikely...'

The Naval Attaché job should have lasted two years, but Kerans was invalided home early, after contracting dysentery. During the summer of 1956, the *Amethyst* finally met her end when Kerans acted as technical adviser on a film about the incident. Originally, the film was to be called *The Sitting Duck* but this was later changed to *Yangtse Incident*. It was directed by Michael Anderson and starred the phlegmatic, firm-chinned Richard Todd (of *Dam Busters* fame) as Kerans. The *Amethyst* re-enacted the scenes of her ordeal for the benefit of the film – with the River Orwell between Ipswich and Harwich serving as the Yangtse.

As ever, Kerans didn't inspire neutral feelings: people either loved him or hated him. The action-unit camera-man was one who took an instant dislike to him, later describing him as 'an arrogant, rude, self-opinionated bore who would listen to no one and to whom film-makers seemed to be a large gang of coolies dragging stones to erect a monument to him'.

HMS *Amethyst* had been taken out of mothballs for the filming but no one had appreciated what bad shape she was in – her engines didn't work and she had to be towed from Devonport to Harwich. The film company advertised in the local papers at Devonport for an engineer to get the ship running again and a Commander Forbes replied. He was interviewed by Kerans, who told the crew that Forbes was an old acquaintance of his, and offered the job. For three days, the engineer worked below decks until at last the bulkhead lights began to glow again and the ship's engines came back to life. Forbes was the hero of the hour but he was a shy man who shunned praise and kept himself to himself below decks. His one request was that no one touch the motor-boat he had tied alongside the ship for his personal use.

One day, Kerans, unable to locate another vessel, ordered that Forbes's motor-boat be used to bring some equipment from the shore to the ship. The normally quiet Forbes exploded when he found out. 'Who gave permission?' he demanded. The whole deck fell silent, shocked by the vehemence of the outburst. 'I did as a matter of fact,' Kerans said. 'How dare you?' Forbes shouted, 'after I have given specific orders. I am the senior officer in this ship and don't you forget it!' A torrent of invective was then heaped on poor Kerans who was visibly embarrassed that this exchange was happening in front of the whole film unit and the ship's company.

With the motor-boat back in place, apologies were made and accepted and filming continued. A few days later, though, Commander Forbes went on shore – with money from the film company's coffers – to order some expensive spare parts he claimed he needed. He checked into a hotel and was promptly arrested, taken to Ipswich Police Station and charged with fraud in connection with some Wimbledon tennis tickets. He was later tried and sentenced to four years' imprisonment. It emerged at the trial that he was a confidence trickster who always took on the identity of a high-ranking person – he had several times been a brigadier and a bishop. Although he had never been in the Royal Navy, he had ended his war service as a corporal in the Royal Electrical and Mechanical Engineers, which was where he had learned about engines. Kerans, it seemed, had claimed to know Forbes because he thought it would look impressive that he had been able to call upon such a high-ranking engineer for the job.

Meanwhile, the *Amethyst* was damaged by an explosion off her port bow during the filming. This dented her bow and holed a fuel tank and Kerans had to give the order to abandon ship. The producer said afterwards, 'We very nearly sank her which was more than the Communists could do.' HMS *Amethyst* was taken back to Plymouth with a ten-degree list and ended her life there, in the graveyard of the ship-breakers.

HRH The Duke of Edinburgh attended the première of the film on 2 April 1957 at the Plaza, London. A couple of months later, in a newspaper interview, Kerans, guessing correctly that the writing was on the wall in terms of his future prospects in the Navy, said with obvious disillusion: 'I'm 42, young enough to make my way in a new industry. I fancy films. So I have put in for some jobs. I'm with Naval Information but there is nothing for me to do – that's the trouble. I've been to about 10 premières of *Yangtse Incident* and I'm getting a bit fed up with it.'

If he had ever wanted to be an admiral, he never mentioned it to anyone – certainly not to his wife (then again, he never mentioned his terrible ordeal on the *Orion,* or his court martial to her, either). He did, though, apply to remain in the Navy, only to have his application turned down. The late 1950s were a difficult time for Kerans. In 1957 his mother died, after a long struggle with cancer. She left him around £30,000, a vast sum in those days, which she had inherited from her godfather, the heir to the Washington-Singer (sewing-machine) fortune. The money helped to pay for his daughters' boarding-school fees and for holidays abroad on which he and his family always travelled first-class.

The next year, under the Compulsory Retirement Scheme, 'Kerans of the *Amethyst*' was axed from the Navy and given a gratuity of £5,500, plus his pension so far earned. With this 'golden bowler' he bought his first house – 26 Riddlesdown Avenue, Purley, Surrey. Stephanie Kerans was stoical: 'It means we shall be moving from Littlehampton to Purley. But I'm not sorry about that. I'm tired of the eternal breeze on the seafront down here.'

The press was still following the couple's every move. In one interview, for the *Daily Express,* Kerans summed up his predicament with rueful bluntness. 'I am looking for a job. I have put an advertisement in the papers. I don't know at the moment what I am going to do. My gratuity from the Service doesn't go far these days and if I don't find a job quickly we shall find it hard to eat. Christmas and the New Year have messed me up a bit because no one ever answers letters around that time.' After the article appeared, he received many letters of sympathy, a typical one, from a Major RC Herbert, read: 'Distressed to read in paper what has happened. My house is open to you.'

Kerans enrolled on a course in business administration. He then found work as a trainee door-to-door insurance salesman with the Sun Alliance Company of Canada, working on commission only. But this, he felt, was demeaning. 'I know of no quicker way to lose your friends than selling pension and life-assurance policies,' he said gloomily. 'Going about knocking on back doors and speaking to people you've never met before is degrading.' He resigned and took a job as a trainee administrative manager with George Wimpey and Co, the building contractors. He was sent to Sunderland to work on the construction of the new steelworks and, while there, was interviewed about his current situation by a reporter from the *Northern Echo*. In the article, Kerans mentioned that he had always been interested in politics.

Kenneth Blake, Conservative agent for the Labour-held seat of the Hartlepools, read the article and rang Kerans up – one Saturday morning while the Commander was in the bath – to ask if he would consider being their prospective parliamentary candidate. Kerans agreed and the newspapers reported the story with headlines about him getting a 'clean start' in politics. He missed his adoption meeting because of a chill.

While he was campaigning, Kerans cannily made sure that all the cinemas in Hartlepool were showing the *Yangtse Incident*. On election night, as crowds watched the results on the *Daily Telegraph* indicator in Piccadilly, a great ovation came with the news of 85-year-old Sir Winston Churchill's return. Kerans's victory, after two counts, got the biggest cheer of the night. He won his seat with 25,463 votes, a majority of just 103 votes over the Labour candidate. The Conservatives won the 1959 election comfortably and Harold Macmillan became Prime Minister.

Kerans's MP's salary and allowance was £1,500. He didn't buy a house in his constituency, but would drive up there and stay as a guest of local prominent Conservatives. The maiden speech of John Kerans, MP concerned the problems that publicans would have to face if they had to draw additional money to cash cheques, thanks to a proposed new Bill. They would lay themselves open to being robbed or knocked on the head, he argued. This went down well, and Kerans got a taste for speaking in the House.

For his journeys north to his constituency, he used to

carry 'extra ballast' in the boot of his car because of the 'strong cross-winds' he experienced on the M1. His second speech in the House, therefore, concerned... the problem of cross-winds on the M1. He called for aluminium bollards to be fitted all the way along the motorway.

A scan through *Hansard* reveals that Kerans had no particular recurring themes, he just liked to champion single-issue causes. He was keen to bring back the birch, for instance, and thought that each convicted person should be given the right to choose for himself between a sentence of corporal punishment and a sentence of detention. Some of his causes seem a little eccentric now. He called for lilos to have lines and stakes attached to them in case children floated out to sea on them. He sought legislation to permit all-in wrestling by women (he'd heard it went on behind a Sussex pub, the Red Lion, and had gone along to watch and found it 'perfectly innocent and amusing'). And he called for the abolition of August bank holidays, as well as for a ban on tattooing for anyone under the age of 18. He also sought to prevent the sale of toy guns that resembled real ones.

But most of his speeches dealt with weighty issues. He asked questions in the House about the shortage of police dogs; protested against imports from Cuba; spoke against seal culling; asked the Postmaster General to use his powers to ensure that the BBC refrained from broadcasting plays detrimental to recruiting for the armed forces; and he spoke out against the use of sex hormones on animals.

Enoch Powell, the Minister of Health, bore the brunt of Kerans's questions. Kerans thought more should be done to ensure that patients discharged from mental hospitals were not a danger to society. He also questioned the minister on what measures were being taken to remove Strontium 90 from dried and natural milk. At his wife's suggestion – Stephanie was by this time a JP and leading pro-abortion campaigner – he demanded that compensation should be given to victims of the drug Distaval (the tradename for thalidomide) and that Powell should take the moral responsibility for having allowed the drug to be given to pregnant women in the first place.

This range of subjects reveals a compassionate man who was prepared stand up to the Whips. He was unassuming, dignified and rarely made any pretence to be clever. And he was always prepared to accept responsibility when things went wrong: on one occasion, he apologised to the House and took the blame when sea cadets were used as a guard of honour at the Digswell Conservative Association garden party, when they were not permitted to take part in political events.

Kerans doesn't seem to have enjoyed many perks from

his term in office, although in 1960 he did join the board of a PR firm. He struck up an acquaintance with the young Margaret Thatcher, who used to lean on his shoulder on the backbenches to listen to the loudspeakers in the backs of the seats, and he enjoyed the socialising that went with being an MP. Once he got drunk on the House of Commons terrace with Vice Admiral Sir Louis le Bailly, with whom he had been at the Royal Naval College, Dartmouth and had served on the ill-fated HMS *Naiad*. On that occasion, he began cheerfully enough but became maudlin and kept recalling the sheer awfulness of his experience onboard HMS *Orion*, a subject which possessed him still.

All in all, Kerans seems to have cut rather a forlorn figure as an MP. Ferdinand Mount, then an assistant to Selwyn Lloyd, now the editor of the *Times Literary Supplement,* who met him at this time, remembers him as a shy, haunted-looking man, who talked haltingly about the problems of unemployment in the North-East.

One night in 1963, Stephanie noticed her husband pacing up and down, as though on a quarter-deck. This is what he did when he was about to make a decision. And he was the sort of person who, once he made his mind up, was resolute. He made an announcement next day. 'I shall not fight another election in the North-East. I don't get any home life.'

There was another reason. He feared that, as Hartlepool was a traditional Labour seat, he would lose his deposit, something he could not afford to do since losing his inherited fortune – after, as he claimed, his private banker had invested it unwisely on his behalf. He added that he would be happy to continue in politics if he was offered a constituency nearer his home. No offers came and three years of unemployment followed. Kerans began to suffer from sinusitis and money became so tight he had to sell his athletics cups. 'I have been on the executive list at the employment exchange for two years and I have advertised for a job but all without success,' he said to a reporter. After giving up politics, he had tried the Stock Exchange, as an assistant to the partners at the stockbrokers, Mitton and Butler. 'That was all right until the Socialists got in in 1964,' he said. 'But then there was just no business at all. I gave it up and I've been kicking my heels ever since. I've put advertisements in the personal columns. I'm prepared to consider almost anything with reasonable prospects...'

In October 1967, he took a job as a bursar at his younger daughter's boarding school, St Michael's at Limpsfield, Surrey. Seven months later he was sacked because he couldn't keep the school's financial affairs in order. 'The bursar's job got very complicated with things like Selective Employment Tax and so on,' he explained to the press. 'Things got into a terrible mess. I had no training for accountancy, you see. The whole thing was quite beyond me. There was much more to it than I realised. You know, collecting fees and so forth.'

Two years later he found a civil service job in the Service Pensions Appeals Tribunal which suited him and gave him much satisfaction. His job was to sift through applications from ex-servicemen, deciding whether or not their claims had merit. He worked in a building off the Tottenham Court Road and commuted in every day from his semi-detached house in Purley.

The Yangtse Incident continued to cast its shadow over his life, of course. Much as he was bored with the story, he was never allowed to bury it. He was still being called upon to give lectures on the subject; still quoted in the press about it. 'I'm heartily sick of discussing China,' he once confided to his wife. When asked to comment on the 25th anniversary of the Incident, he said: 'I have lost interest in it. I knew very well that Thursday was the anniversary. But I am not planning any kind of cele-bration. It all seems a horribly long time back. I am that much older – 59 – time has passed by rapidly. Anyway, the new generation isn't interested. I admit I do miss the sea but I can't do anything about it now. I used to belong to a sailing club but that was too expensive so I gave it up.'

When, 30 years after the Incident, in 1980, China

finally agreed to the appointment of a new British Naval Attaché, Kerans was asked to comment. He was also interviewed for a regional television documentary about the Incident and, looking frail and sounding short of breath, he dutifully delivered his tried and tested line: 'I was one of the few commanders who 24 hours after taking control was told to sink his ship.'

This was also the year in which John Kerans retired, at the age of 65, and moved to a terraced house in Oxted, Surrey. Here he hung his watercolours of naval ships on the wall and considered writing his memoirs. But he settled for going to the odd concert, drinking his favourite tipple, whisky and water, and solving the *Times* crossword each day. He was also able to devote more time to walking his beloved Jack Russell terrier, Algy.

Though he always regretted not having a son, he derived great pleasure in retirement from seeing more of his two daughters. Charmian had become an estate agent and was married to a man who worked for a missing persons charity. Her relationship with her father had always been made difficult by his absence in her youth. Melanie was the apple of her father's eye. She had become a dressmaker who listed Princess Anne among her clients, and was married to a stockbroker. Melanie had two daughters for whom Kerans felt great affection.

But, though he kept his own counsel, it was clear he

wasn't a happy man in old age. He was tormented by the thought that he should have gone on to greater things in the Navy after the Yangtse Incident. Egomania being the strange bedfellow of insecurity and lassitude, his moods would swing between self-belief and self-doubt. This was understandable. When the British public had needed a hero, he had accepted the role with dignity and poise; he had played up and played the game. But he hadn't found it easy living up to the reputation foisted upon him. Sometimes, he had felt like an impostor. He was aware that many of his fellow officers had shared this view – and that many more hadn't been able to forgive him his fame.

According to Melanie, he was a generous, amusing and sentimental man who never forgot a birthday. But he could also be dogmatic, cantankerous and intolerant of the shortcomings of others. In later life his partial deafness – the result of too many years' exposure to gunfire – made him irascible and frustrated, especially in a crowded room.

After only three years of retirement, John Kerans was diagnosed with cancer of the bowel. Not long after this was reversed he developed cancer of the throat. He saw a specialist who recommended he went to Crawley Hospital for an operation. But, sadly, a consultant at the hospital decided that the cancer had already spread too far. All they could do was give him a throat tube, the size of a little finger. Stephanie had to purée all his food and, by August

1985, Kerans found he was losing so much strength he could hardly move.

One day he told Stephanie: 'I can't go on. You'll have to get me into a hospital.' An ambulance arrived and Kerans was carried out of his house on a stretcher and taken to Oxted hospital. He died five days later, at the age of 70. It was a rather ignominious end for the Last Action Hero of the British Empire. That night, his death was the lead item on the BBC current affairs programme *Newsnight*.

His funeral service was held at St Peter's, Tandridge, a couple of miles away from his house in Oxted. The church was full, with many former crew members of the *Amethyst* in attendance, as well as members of the local cricket team, of which he was president. Algy, his Jack Russell, came along, too. Kerans is buried in a quiet corner of the churchyard, his grave planted with begonias.

In Greek mythology, a hero was a man of superhuman qualities favoured by the gods. Kerans wasn't quite one of those, but he was a courageous warrior. His gravestone is made of Portland stone, which, because it is porous, is tinged green from the holly tree above it. The inscription reads: 'In loving memory of Commander John Simon Kerans DSO RN. Captain of HMS Amethyst 1949. June 30 1915 – September 12 1985.'

ACKNOWLEDGEMENTS

Mrs Stephanie Kerans; Charmian Barttelot; Melanie Baker; Vice Adm Sir Louis le Bailly; Vice Adm Sir Peter Berger; Rear Adm Colin Dunlop; Cdr David Hunter; Lt Cdr Gerald Craig-McFeely; Lt Cdr Stuart Hett and Lt Cdr Alan Tyler.

BIBLIOGRAPHY

Lawrence Earl: *Yangtse Incident* (Harrap, 1950)
CE Lucas Phillips: *Escape of the Amethyst* (Heinemann, 1957)
Vice Adm Sir Louis le Bailly: *A Man Around the Engine* (Kenneth Mason, 1990)
Malcolm H Murfett: *Hostage on the Yangtse* (Naval Institute Press, 1992)
Lt Cdr Alan Tyler: *Cheerful and Contented* (Book Guild, 2000)

Nigel Farndale is a feature writer and columnist for the Sunday Telegraph Magazine *and was named Interviewer of the Year at the British Press Awards 2000. His first novel,* A Sympathetic Hanging, *is published in paperback in 2001. He is married, with two sons, and lives in London.*